PULP
Literature

Also from Pulp Literature Press

The Beer Fairy Issue, 1
The Killer Teddy Bear Issue, 2
The Youth Hostels of Faerie Issue, 3
The Icarus Fallen Issue, 4
The Fondly Remembered Magic Issue, 5
The Pesky Summer Jobs Issue, 6
The Fallen Angel Issue, 7
The Albert Ball on Galactic Shore Leave Issue, 8
The Dieselpunk Explorers Issue, 9
The Doesn't Know She's Small Issue, 10
The Allaigna's Song Issue, 11
The Story Teller Issue, 12
The Shadow Issue, 13
The Blue Skies Issue, 14

Stella Ryman and The Fairmount Manor Mysteries
forthcoming March 2017

Allaigna's Song: Overture
forthcoming May 2017

And onwards ...

Good books for the price of a beer!

Thirty Days Towards
An Extraordinary Volume

THE WRITER'S
BOON COMPANION

Mel Anastasiou

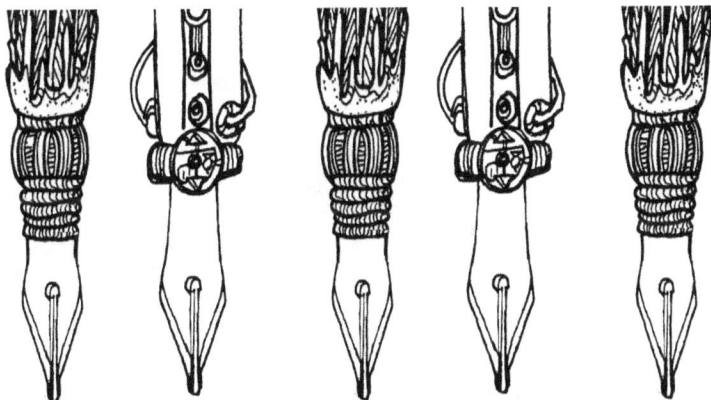

Pulp Literature Press, 2016

ISBN: 978-0-9949565-4-5

Book design and artwork by the author.
Cover design: Rachel Kuo & Mel Anastasiou

Printed and bound in the USA

Published in Canada by Pulp Literature Press
www.pulpliterature.com

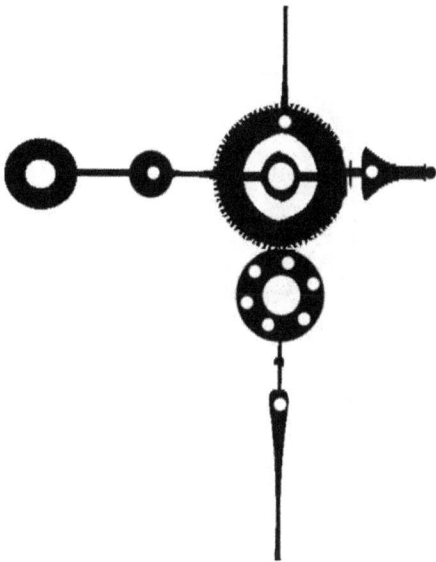

Thinking of
Sir Arthur Conan Doyle,
Jules Verne, William Gibson,
China Miéville and
Neal Stephenson

*H*OW TO USE THIS BOOK

The Writer's Boon Companion is a quiet, thoughtful chap. Boon offers daily hints and exercises to support your narrative along its road to completion. You'll also find generous servings of motivation and philosophy to help you forge ahead over thirty days of drafting towards a completed novel or novella.

The thirty days may be profitably spread out over a longer writing period.

The author using this reflective journal may wish to draft between the pages; that is, for every day in the book, drafting 2,000 to 3,000 words to a cogent outline will get you your novella or short novel in short order. For briefer or longer works, multiply or divide as wisdom dictates.

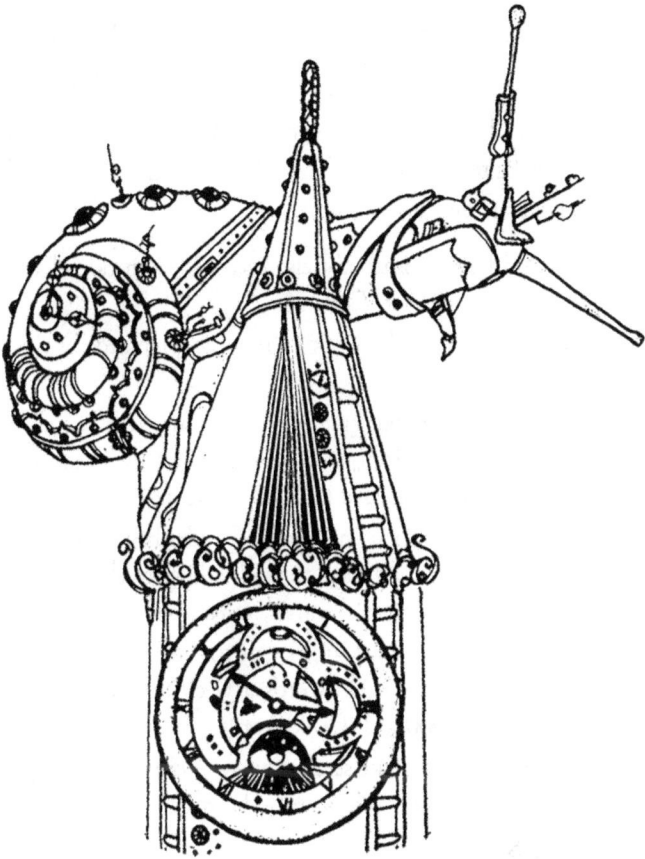

"The game is afoot!"

Arthur Conan Doyle
The Adventures of Sherlock Holmes

AROUND YOUR MANUSCRIPT IN 30 DAYS

A Stimulating Writing Adventure, for Which You, Like Phineas Fogg, Have What It Takes.

All professions have aspects in common, and one of these is waking up in the night to ask yourself, "Do I have what it takes?" You can be sure you'll succeed as a writer if...

1. You read that somebody else has sold a truckload of books and you think, *Fantastic.*

2. You show up for the work every week, prepared for the job.

3. You read up on your craft with the same kind of energy and interest doctors and lawyers do if they want to succeed. For writers, that includes marketing.

4. Your desire is strong enough that you're happy to take five minutes here and there through a busy week to write an outline for a story, a character, and a scene.

5. You are happy to carve out the one to three hours it takes to draft 1,500 to 3,000 words a week to that outline, giving you 70,000 to 140,000 words a year.

6. You are happy to take seven years or more to learn your profession, and you are determined to keep learning.

7. You notice, while you're drafting, revising, or polishing, that you smile from time to time.

8. You love the people you work with: your characters.

9. You love the people you work for: your readers.

With these attitudes and practices, you prosper, rich in persistence and endurance. Furthermore, you can be sure that inspiration will thrive. Your work becomes everything you dream it can be.

Rather the way the airship's captain checks his compass, you may wish here to write your vision for the final scene of your story.

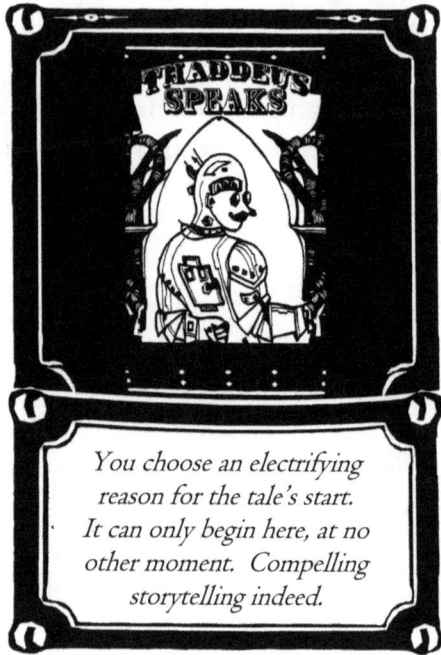

THADDEUS SPEAKS

You choose an electrifying reason for the tale's start. It can only begin here, at no other moment. Compelling storytelling indeed.

2

It may be useful to ascertain that your opening paragraph encompasses time, place, tone, the promise of genre, and a hint at the central conflict.

This may be an admirable moment to list the goals for your next five gripping tales.

4

May I suggest you set out a baker's half-dozen things wrong, at the start, in your protagonist's inner and outer life?

I see that your paragraph one offers your readers a hint at the central conflict, time, setting, tone of voice and the promise of genre. A spectacular start.

5

You may desire at this point
to write down your story goal.

6

May I propose that you state the gist of the story in a single word?

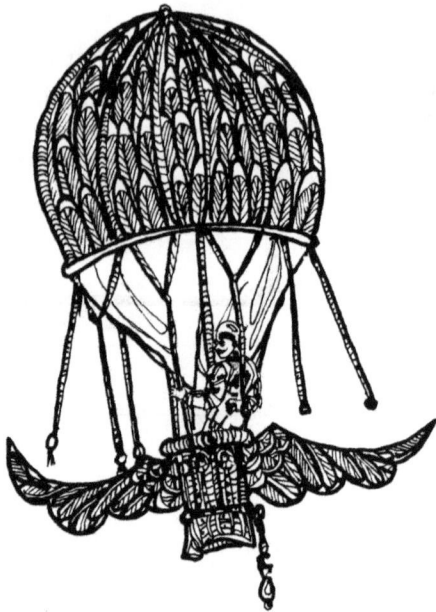

You cleverly employ a supporting character to state the theme of your tale in its first act. What superb storytelling skill!

May I ask, are you planning sequels for this story?

AROUND YOUR MANUSCRIPT IN 30 DAYS

On the Employment of Worthy and Unworthy Companions

Supporting characters can say with charm, or the complete lack of charm, what the protagonist can't or won't. But their magic goes deeper than that. Here are three steps farther than snappy dialogue ...

1. We should hear a supporting character state the theme of the story early on, as in Robert Sawyer's brilliant "Fallen Angel", where the father tells his daughter Angela that there is nothing to fear. "We'll be so high up we'll catch God's eye." But Angela does fear, and the story turns on her fear and what she does because of it.

2. Supporting characters force the protagonist to show readers his or her heroic qualities in contrast with their less heroic aspects. They make sure we don't miss the hero's flaws, either. Take a look at the many Brothers who have taken the black on the Wall in GRR Martin's *Game of Thrones* series. Their leader Jon Snow is so remarkably steadfast and true that it takes an army of supporting characters to bring out his weaknesses.

3. In the case of Sherlock Holmes, it is less his clients than his challengers who stir him from doldrums and depression to become the man we all need him to be. Supporting characters at their best force the protagonist and antagonist to make choices they would not have faced on their own, no matter how stubborn or brave they might be.

"Which path do you intend to take, Nell?" said the
Constable, sounding very interested.
"Conformity or rebellion?"
"Neither one, both ways are simple-minded —
they are only for people who cannot cope with
contradiction and ambiguity."

Neal Stephenson
*The Diamond Age:
Or, a Young Lady's Illustrated Primer*

This might be an excellent time to write your goals for the rest of this calendar year.

_____

_____

_____

_____

_____

_____

_____

_____

Every goal you write takes you a step closer to your grand and astonishing dreams.

Your perfectly flawed and magnetic protagonist immediately captures our favour with a small sacrifice in your first chapter. Your readers, like Conan Doyle's, will press for more.

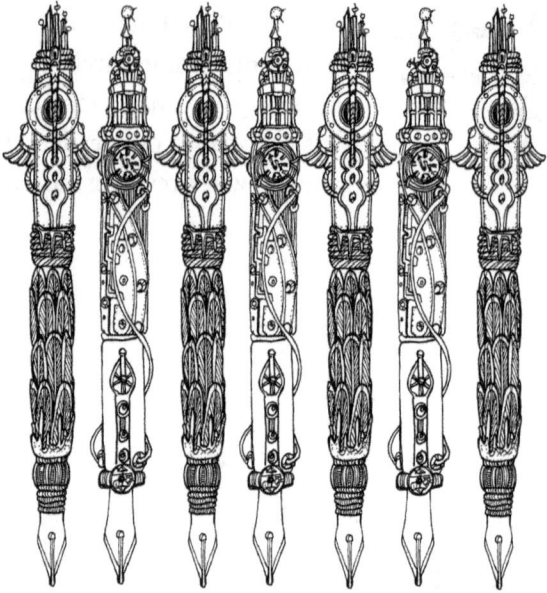

If you like, you might reflect upon your work in Act I, remembering how you arrived at your ideas for the harbinger of change: a small kindness by which your admirably flawed character wins the reader's loyalty; a mentor's wise words; your hero's refusal; debate; and the choice that propels this same hero into Act II.

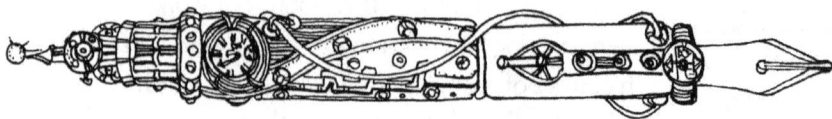

AROUND YOUR MANUSCRIPT IN 30 DAYS
On Crafting a Ripping Tale and Slashing Revision Time

You can live your full-time writer's life along with your full-time working and personal life. Addressing key points in your manuscript during your non-drafting time is one way to manage it.

For example, posit that your second act is filled with energy, jam-packed with trials and learning for your protagonist and allies. One of the reasons this section of your tale succeeds so well is that you dig deep for ideas. Maybe you take a couple of minutes to make a list of adventures, digging past obvious ideas into the intriguing ones.

These few minutes of hard thinking are worth hours or even days of revision, for with this sort of planning each adventure you write causes your characters to grow and change as they attempt feats and make connections they never would have faced in Act I. In this way, character development is built right in as you go, and your story grows in strength along with your reader's enjoyment.

Your career is right on track. Have another wonderful day in your Writer's Life.

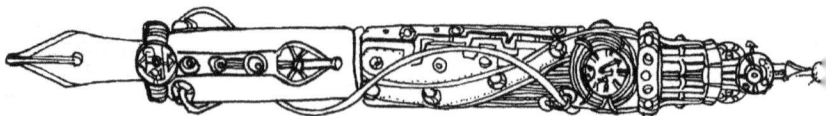

It may please you to ruminate upon the skills your hero is gaining, and what choices forced the learning.

Legions of readers agree, your plan for supporting characters and events that force increasingly impossible choices unquestionably takes the biscuit.

Have I mentioned how much I enjoy your writing voice? Distinctive and engaging. An indisputable winner.

The first discipline that goals create is that of penning them into being. All else follows accordingly.

THADDEUS SPEAKS

What admirable work you are up to in the line of character development. I observe that you show it through the way the hero deals with setbacks.

A suggestion to help with Act II: consider where you might place moments of beauty and peace here and there, so we may see how your characters are growing and have changed in the course of their adventures.

AROUND YOUR MANUSCRIPT IN 30 DAYS
Just as for Sherlock Holmes, Study and Natural Talent Hold Our Compass Steady

We've all met great teachers, superb doctors, topnotch lawyers, successful authors, and each of these have something in common. No matter what challenges they face, they love their work and toil to improve their skills and insights. Interest is the chief sign of talent in any field, for if we are interested, we work hard no matter how tough the learning gets. Those of us who proceed, succeed.

Writing fiction is especially challenging because all readers are experts in storytelling. They may not be able to explain what makes a perfectly readable tale, but every reader knows it when it's there.

Luckily, we writers are equipped with the same clever inner expert. As well, each of us comes to the writing table with certain skills that come easily to us. Most of us have other skills that we need to develop. What matters is our willingness to carry on. All craft may be learned if the interest is there.

Interest, focus, a love of the work and the learning that goes with it: these are some of the most reliable indicators of a writer's talent, and are certainly the easiest to recognize in ourselves.

"I looked on, I thought, I reflected, I admired, in a state of stupefaction not altogether mingled with fear!"

Jules Verne
Journey to the Centre of the Earth

15

Have you considered writing down ways that your hero's darkest hour may become even more dire?

16 Just now you may find it a suitable moment to check back on your narrative's events to be sure that things don't just happen to your protagonist, but ensue from that character's choices.

_____

_____

_____

_____

_____

_____

Your mastery of uplift is spellbinding.
These shining moments make the darkness
more terrifying.

A valuable exercise at this point in time may be to check the inner and outer negatives you wrote down on Day 4. How many of these have been addressed thus far? Which remain?

It may be desirable to write out your own achievements in self-motivation and time management. What are five goals for establishing these practices in your writing life?

As you write your goals, make them as charismatic and fantastic as your dreams.

Might I recommend writing out your vision for the final showdown? You may find it useful to list moves and countermoves.

Extraordinary, the way you manage to carve out the time to work on your manuscript through your busy week. Astounding discipline.

It may be of practical benefit to write out your excellent plan for resolving what we may call your protagonist's primary relationship.

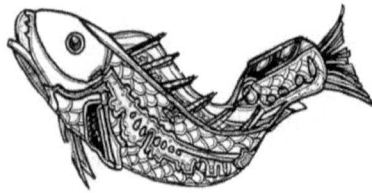

AROUND YOUR MANUSCRIPT IN 30 DAYS
A Mathematical Construction of Stimulating Possibilities

If we want to lead full-time writing careers in our full-time lives, consider the happy mathematics of writing books.

Writers talk about books taking six months or a year. Or, indeed, years. And of course any profession will fill the entire time we give it, including every hour of every day, if we allow the work to schedule us instead of the other way around.

But, step back and look at the time it takes us to write, rather than the time it takes a book to get itself written, and we find that it's possible to write about a thousand to fifteen hundred words in an hour, so long as we know what we're going to write.

We're going to be outlining, revising, polishing, and planning our marketing strategies during the week. But unlike drafting, these necessary activities can be slotted into smaller time frames.

If those fifteen hundred words are based on a solid outline, then they will become part of the book, and nothing is wasted. Write to this outline twice a week for about an hour each sitting, and the outcome will be about three thousand words. (Mind you, if you are happy to take five hours to compose a perfect paragraph, then carry on, and don't mind me).

A serviceable practice may be to list the negative circumstances you noted at the start, and how and when your hero has overcome or, more interestingly, overturned them throughout Acts II and III.

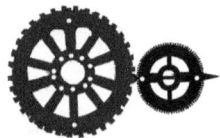

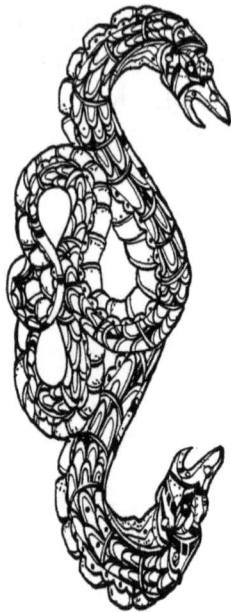

"In an infinite universe, all may become real sooner or later. Yet it is always up to mankind to make real what it really wishes to be real."

Michael Moorcock
The Warlord of the Air

22. I'd be interested to know, how does your protagonist become a new person after your story's darkest hour? Fascinating storytelling.

_____

_____

_____

_____

_____

_____

_____

_____

_____

_____

You toil so hard on behalf of your loyal readers. Commendable spirit and drive on your part.

You may wish to write down your five-year plan for writing, year by year. What a splendid vista of accomplishment, I must say.

At this point you will no doubt wish to plan the hint at future conflict that you'll weave into the story's ending.

Today I was looking into the future to read reviews of your work. You'll be chuffed to know that they're excellent. Here's one of my favourites: "Captivating throughout." Congratulations.

You will certainly find it to your advantage to write the story once more in a single sentence. [*The Protagonist*] struggles against [*the Antagonist*] to achieve [*the Story Goal*] in spite of [*Obstacles, Inner & Outer*].

Your hard work shows in your own satisfaction with it, as well as your readers' loyalty and pleasure.

26 One task of practical benefit may be to search out and shoot with duelling pistols all exclamation marks except those following interjections.

Perhaps you will keep to your working title, but it may be expedient just now to write out twenty possible titles for your story, just to test whether there's another candidate lurking around the corner. Or maybe the title for your sequel.

Your hero takes a different path towards the final section of your tale, perhaps even an opposite path to the one we all anticipated, to achieve the story goal. Clever plotting.

When you write your goals, smile, because each one is your wish come true.

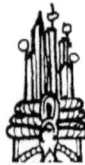

AROUND YOUR MANUSCRIPT IN 30 DAYS
A Zeppelin's-eye View of the New Writing World

It's easy to identify obstacles to success in writing in the new world of publishing. However, against every obstacle, we can weigh the opportunities.

For most of us, it's more difficult than ever to make it in the world of traditional publishing. But if our work is so good that it's already moved beyond 'publishable' to 'irresistible', then once a book is traditionally published, our opportunities to sell our work are legion. Thirty years ago we might have booked school and library visits, a few bookstore signings, and hoped for a good review in *Quill and Quire*. Not so bad, but today a traditionally published author can give writing seminars online to the world, connect with readers through Goodreads, and do guest blog tours across the continent to reach new readers.

For those of us who want to succeed in independent publishing, again the opportunities are many and clear. For example, distribution is no longer an issue. True, we have to look for ways to make our work visible in the sea of writers on the independent scene. But each of these authors is a reader, and, thankfully, they are also colleagues with whom we tend to cooperate more than compete. What Hugh Howey with *Wool* and Andy Weir with *The Martian* have accomplished through talent, determination, and diligence may help us see how to build our own careers on our own terms.

Take a large enough view of the field of writing, and all those obstacles spell out the news: there has never been a better time to be a writer.

A constructive exercise occurs to me: to visit the beginnings of each of your chapters, ensuring that you've touched on time, place, genre, and a hint at the central conflict.

What a clever hero you have written. Flawed but clever. I remember how pleased dear Verne was to work with such characters. You're in good company.

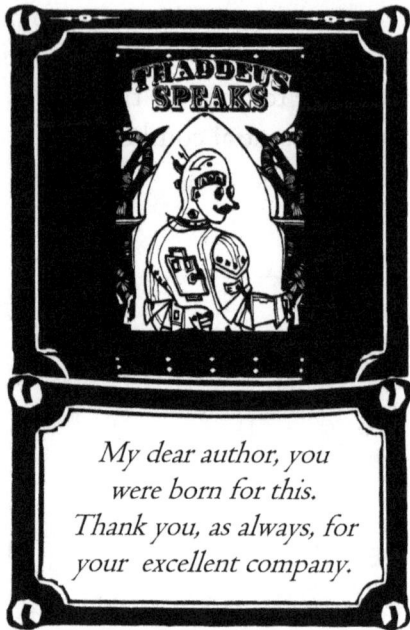

THADDEUS SPEAKS

*My dear author, you
were born for this.
Thank you, as always, for
your excellent company.*

Like the Invisible Man of HG Wells, you can celebrate the end of your thirty days by lifting a glass of something bubbly and dancing around your roll-top desk.

ℛEVISIONS CHECKLIST

- ❑ Your opening image resonates with your closing image.
- ❑ Your first paragraph nails time, tone of voice, setting, promise of genre, and a hint at the central conflict.
- ❑ You identify at least four negatives, inner and outer, in your protagonist's life.
- ❑ A character states the theme of your tale early on.
- ❑ You can write the story goal in a single sentence.
- ❑ Your hero gains skills and knowledge in Act II that will be vital to the showdown.
- ❑ Events and supporting characters force impossible choices upon the hero.
- ❑ Your antagonist believes in his or her own struggle.
- ❑ Your antagonist is also gaining skills and knowledge.
- ❑ You place moments of beauty throughout Act II, so that hero and supporting characters may reflect on how they've grown and changed.
- ❑ As you enter Act III, your hero has a different, perhaps even opposite, plan to achieve the story goal.
- ❑ Every possible character is heading for the final showdown.
- ❑ You've included a hint at future conflict at the end of your story.
- ❑ Revisions include clearing dialogue of tags and description, to examine exchanges of power.
- ❑ Each chapter beginning settles the reader in with time, setting, promise of genre, and hint at the conflict.
- ❑ You've checked the end of chapters and removed sentences that feel like story endings.

"My sustenance is information.
My interventions are hidden.
I increase as I learn. I compute, so I am."

China Miéville
Perdido Street Station

PULP *Literature*
WRITING CONTESTS

The Bumblebee Flash Fiction Contest
For previously unpublished works of
fiction up to 750 words in length
January 15 through February 15

The Magpie Award for Poetry
For previously unpublished
poems up to 100 lines
March 15 through April 15

The Hummingbird Prize for Flash Fiction
For previously unpublished works of
fiction up to 1000 words
May 15 through Jun 15

The Raven Short Story Contest
For previously unpublished short
fiction between 500 and 2500
words in length
September 15 through October 15

ABOUT THE AUTHOR

Mel Anastasiou loves her writing life in the UK and BC. She is a senior acquisitions editor with Pulp Literature Press, and writes mysteries starring sleuths who are often fish out of water and gifted amateur detectives. Mel can be found every day writing and drawing, walking for miles to look at inspired Victorian architecture, and dreaming of steam-powered robots.

For news on the **Hertfordshire Pub Mysteries**, the **Fairmount Manor Mysteries**, and the **Monument Studios Mysteries**, you're invited to follow melanastasiou.wordpress.com

For more **Writing Guides** and **ripping good stories** find our shop at pulpliterature.com.

www.ingramcontent.com/pod-product-compliance
Lightning Source LLC
Chambersburg PA
CBHW070801050426
42452CB00012B/2436